May our heart's garden of awakening bloom with hundreds of flowers.

-Thich Nhat Hanh

Journal writing can open you to a greater understanding of yourself, increase your awareness, and lead to greater clarity and effectiveness. Throughout this journal, let Thich Nhat Hanh's compassionate messages about life provide guidance and inspiration for your own inner journey.

Vietnamese Zen master, Thich Nhat Hanh, is a teacher, scholar, and peace activist who lectures throughout the world and writes on the practice of mindfulness and peaceful living. His dedication to peace and his consummate understanding of the human condition make him one of the world's most admired spiritual leaders.

May our heart's garden of
awakening bloom with hundreds of flowers.

A halo of wisdom spreads in every direction,
enveloping all with love and compassion, joy and equanimity.

This body is not me. I am not limited by this body. I am life without boundaries.

KIRSTEN

KIRSTEN

KIRSTEN

KIRSTEN

KIRSTEN

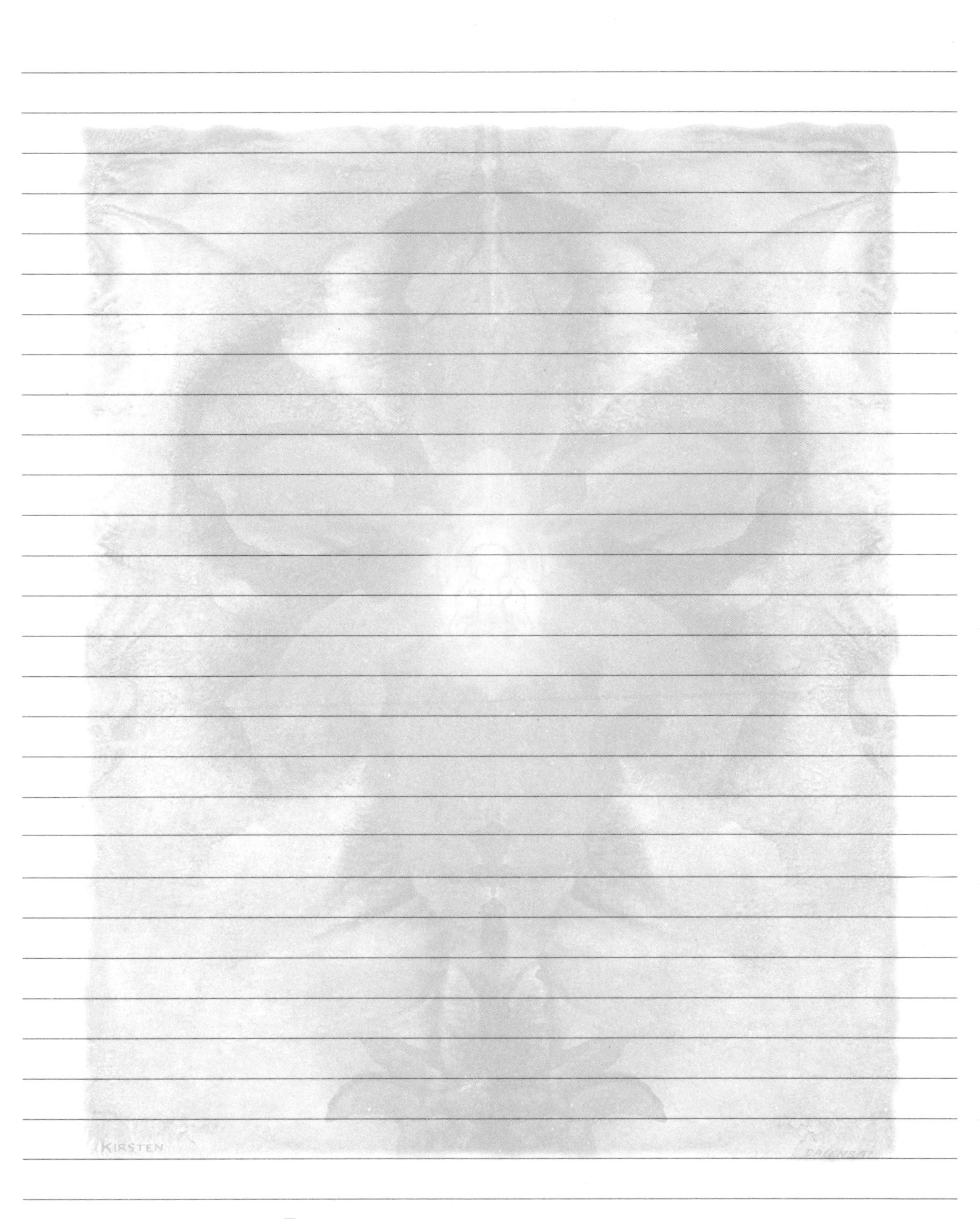

Birth and death are only doors through which
we must pass, sacred thresholds on our journey.

KIRSTEN

KIRSTEN

KIRSTEN

KIRSTEN

KIRSTEN

We will meet today. We will meet tomorrow.

We will meet at the source every moment.

KIRSTEN

KIRSTEN

KIRSTEN

KIRSTEN

Knowing that words can create happiness or suffering, I am determined to speak truthfully, with words that inspire self-confidence, joy, and hope.

Taking refuge in the Buddha in myself, I aspire to help all people recognize their own awakened nature, realizing the mind of love.

Living beings are birthless, pure, and silent from the beginning.

This is the Practice of the Highest understanding

When the river of mind is truly calm,

the moon is refleted perfectly upon the surface of the deep waters.

N. KIRSTEN

Trees have their roots and water has its source. We know that you, our ancestors, are our roots and we are your continuation.

Here is the impermanent and yet continuously flowing world.

Let us stand together for future generations.

N. KIRSTEN
HONSHU

Vow to offer joy to one person in the morning, and to help relieve the grief of one person in the afternoon.

Vow to let go of all worry and anxiety in order to be light and free.

Each moment you are alive is a gem,
shining through and containing earth and sky, water and clouds.

However much we have drifted on the ocean of suffering, today we see clearly that there is a beautiful path. We turn toward the light of loving kindness to direct us.

Walk and touch peace every moment.

Walk and touch happiness every moment.

Cherish this very moment.

Let go of the stream of distress and embrace life fully in your arms.